Phonics Bible Stories

The

The Modest King

Claudia Courtney ☆ Illustrated by Bill Clark

CPH®
SAINT LOUIS

For Heidi.
"Enter His gates with thanksgiving
and His courts with praise; give thanks
to Him and praise His name."
(Psalm 100:4 NIV)

Copyright © 1999 Concordia Publishing House
3558 S. Jefferson Avenue, St. Louis, MO 63118-3968
Manufactured in the United States of America

1 2 3 4 5 6 7 8 9 10   08 07 06 05 04 03 02 01 00 99

Note to Grown-ups

The love of reading is one of the greatest things you can instill in your child. It opens new horizons, exposes your child to new ideas, and provides information as well as entertainment.

This beginning reader series blends the best of two worlds—phonics to help your child learn to read and popular Bible stories to help your child learn to read God's Word. After you use a book in this series, open your child's Bible and read the story from God's Word. Emphasize to your child that this story is not make-believe—it's true, and we can believe every word in God's Holy Book.

Before you begin, review together the word, sound, and spelling list on page 16. This story emphasizes the phoneme which makes the short ŏ sound as heard in the words *clop* and *donkey*.

After your review, read the story to your child, exaggerating the designated phonetic sound or sounds. Discuss the illustrations. Your enthusiasm for reading, and especially for reading God's Word, should be contagious. Run your finger under each word as you read it, showing your child that it is the words that convey the actual story. Have your child join with you in reading repeated phrases.

Finally, have your child read the story as you offer plenty of praise. Pause to allow your youngster time to sound out words, but provide help when necessary to avoid frustration. When a mistake is made, invite your child to reread the sentence. This provides an appropriate opportunity to guide your early reader.

Please remember that your child is learning and blending a complex set of new skills. Early success and your generous praise are keys to opening the door to your child's world of reading, especially to the joys of reading the Bible.

Claudia Courtney

Clip clop, clip clop.
The donkey plodded along
the rocky sod.

Clip clop, clip clop.
The donkey plodded along
with Jesus on top.

5

Clip clop, clip clop.
Jesus was on His way to the
city.

People had flocked to the
city.
People had flocked to see
Jesus.

Clip clop, clip clop.
The donkey trod along the
city street.

Flop plop, flop drop.
The people tossed cloth and
branches as Jesus crossed on
the donkey.

Flop plop, flop drop.
The people blocked the
street as the donkey trod
along.

The people stopped to
honor Jesus.
The people offered praises
and songs to God.

Clip clop, clip clop.
Jesus nodded at the throng
as the donkey plodded
along.

Scoff scoff, scoff scoff.
Mockers spotted Jesus and
wanted Him gone.

Scoff scoff, scoff scoff.
Mockers were shocked at
the Modest King who
was God's Son.

14

Mockers plotted to rob Jesus
of praises and songs.
But, on that day, praise for
Jesus was strong.

Word Lists

phoneme ŏ

along	honor	shocked
blocked	mockers	sod
clop	modest	Son
cloth	nodded	songs
crossed	offered	spotted
donkey	on	stopped
drop	plodded	strong
flocked	plop	throng
flop	plotted	top
God	rob	tossed
God's	rocky	trod
gone	scoff	

Other Words

and	for	praise	was
as	had	praises	way
at	Him	see	were
branches	His	street	who
but	Jesus	the	with
city	King	that	
clip	of	to	
day	people	wanted	